PEACE
IN A WORLD OF
PIZZA

TOM HART

iUniverse LLC
Bloomington

Peace In A World Of Pizza

iUniverse books may be ordered through booksellers or by contacting:

iUniverse LLC
1663 Liberty Drive
Bloomington, IN 47403
www.iuniverse.com
1-800-Authors (1-800-288-4677)

ISBN: 978-1-4917-0536-0 (sc)
ISBN: 978-1-4917-0537-7 (ebk)

Library of Congress Control Number: 2013915436

Printed in the United States of America

iUniverse rev. date: 08/27/2013

Pick up the book and an original peaceful
message will be delivered!

This is a cookbook for all ages and a global message of peace for everyone. It's about great pizza making and exploring the globe of flavorful ingredients. Come into a world of peace and a world of adventure.

What kind of pizza do you like?

It would be great to solve world peace by cooking dinner. Now you can. Everyone enjoys a nice slice of pizza once in a while. This book will give you great ideas on how to make the best pizza while finding true peace within yourself. It is time for the world to enjoy a delicious peace of pizza. The ins and outs of making the best dough and sauce are made so simply. It is your personal choice to put any toppings on your pizza. In this book, Chef Tomato will guide you on making the dough, making the sauce and taking toppings to a whole new level. May peace be with the world.

THIS BOOK WILL GUIDE YOU AND YOUR FRIENDS TO GATHER TOGETHER AND MAKE A DELICIOUS PIZZA. A BIG PIZZA PARTY FOR EVERYONE.

Here on Earth: We All Stand Together

The secret to world peace is the ability to be kind. Kindness will allow you to touch one's soul. Believing in yourself is crucial to love one another. This will lead to kind actions for all.

We are all on Earth to be loved and make differences in people. Keep your dreams coming true and forever there will be joy.

We must allow ourselves to respect all walks of life if we want to have unity in this world.

The secret to peace is the ability to be kind, loving, and caring. If everyone joins together and delivers strength, the world will be one step closers to peace.

Just Say Planet Pizzeria!

Become someone and they will see how easy it is to become a star in this universe. Make it before you bake it!

Making pizza is just as easy as making peace. For pizza you need dough, sauce, and toppings. For peace you need understanding, sincerity, and love.

Thank You

A special thanks should be directed to all of my family. They have guided the way for my success and should feel special we are all one.

The friends that I have chosen closely make my daily activities worthwhile and for that they receive a great amount of recognition.

Also, those who have decided to read the book and make the recipes receive much merit as well.

INTRODUCTION

Just like pizza, peace can be anything you want it to be. Whether you want international ingredients such as Asian, European, Middle Eastern, Latin, or American foods, pizza is an open canvas of ideas. Pizza toppings are very trendy and can be very liberal. Feel free to top your pizza with whatever you like.

Imagine a peaceful world. A world without stress, horror or war. Be great and all can enjoy wonderful pizza.

Be ready for the adventure of CHEF Tomato

This book will give you great ideas on how to make the best pizza while finding true inner peace. It is time for the world to enjoy a delicious peace of pizza. The ins and outs of making the best dough and sauce are so simple. It is your personal choice to put any toppings on your pizza pie.

In this book Chef Tomato will guide you through making the dough, rolling the dough, and taking toppings to a whole new level.

Tom Hart

PEACE IN A World of PIZZA

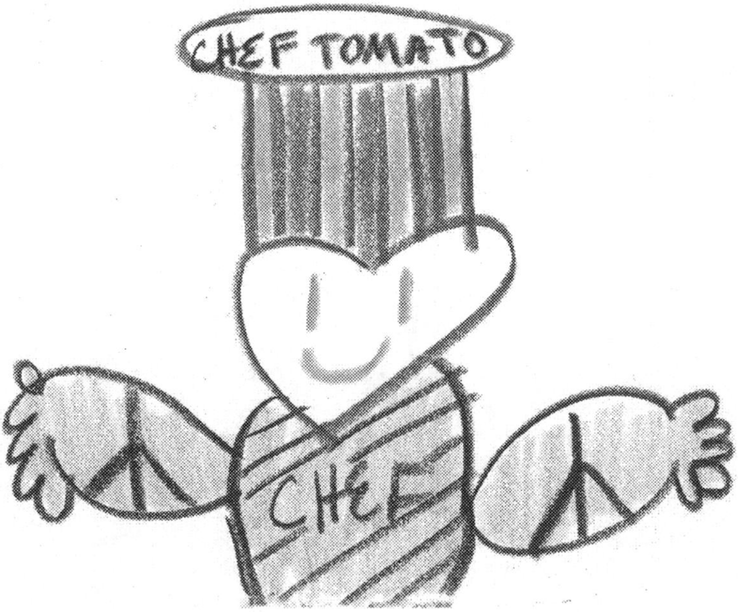

The Peace Poem

"The Rise Of World Peace"

From the stars to the sea, a

Beautiful day goes by.

The sea shines the reflection of our dreams.

Will they come true?

We have to live out our dream

That we all live in.

When the time is right, we will all

Have freedom. The time to live breaks a new sunrise. A rise

To all for freedom.

It is not about fighting anymore

But rather to have peace on

Earth. To know we all live in heaven and we must respect

Our nature, ourselves and our heavenly dream.

But furthermore respect everything and everyone.

We shall have peace only if our

Dreams are to have freedom

Please be yourself and live in peace

On earth for we do not know what life will bring?

Allow us to live in a world of one

We can live peacefully together and independently from each other.

A world of peace is a world of freedom.

The Pizza Poem

"Being Ready 2 Serve"

Now you're using the skills to cook,

Read and enjoy this culinary book.

The pizza is rising and it's time to take look.

You are the one entering the game,

This could be your ticket to food fame,

Listen to the words of wisdom in the world to make your claim.

We all need to be kind to each other and smile,

Flip that dough and stay in the kitchen for just a while,

Make the pizza and enjoy a milkshake from you recipe file.

Let your heart guide your way and put your pizza in,

Watch the happiness you get from everyone's chin,

This could be your first big win!

Well we all will compete but will shake hands,

This is the time to make your pizza to the stands,

Deliver a kind friend a peaceful treat for all the lands.

A Though Of Inspiration

Days just pass by like the clouds in the air. The people should try to enjoy a nice slice of pizza whenever they can. It is all about being kind to everyone. Let us take the step of peacefulness with every breath. It is not too often that we hear the words of wisdom to be nice to each other. It is time to make the peace of pizza everyone will enjoy.

To care and love

Teach yourself to be the best. Teach yourself to be caring. Teach yourself to love.

Life is too short. Keep your life simple and rewards shall come. Believe in yourself and be the best.

Be kind to one another and peace will fill the air. Kindness is the root of peace.

Take upon every opportunity to be charming to one another and good karma will come your way.

This is the Key. It was nice to meet you. Now let's all be free.

Developing culinary skills will teach you how to follow directions.

Love and peace are the answers to freedom

Imagine a life of greatness and a world of hope.

It is essential to be nice. Believe what comes around, goes around.

Peace in a World of Pizza

Time to Start! It's your life: choose your toppings wisely and enjoy the flavors of the world.

Time to Start! **It's your life: choose your toppings wisely and enjoy the flavors of the world.**

Thin, Thick, Deep Dish or Flat Bread. A crust that all can enjoy. Make your own and you will be delivered with a pleasant treat that millions of people daily.

Read, Look and Cook. It's easy to Make and Eat. So take upon the challenge of becoming a master pizza maker. May all have a slice and be very nice. Now that's Peace of Pizza.

ABC's

A -Achieve Actions

B -Believe in the Business

C -Construct Classics

D -Deliver a Destiny of Dynasties & Deliciousness

E -Everyone Enjoy

F -Fantastic Fun

G -Give Greatness

H -Have Hope

I   -Include Inspiration

J -Jump for Joy

K -Kindness

L -Live a Life of Love

M -Make Milkshakes your Masterpiece

O -Organize Original Opportunities

P -Place a Peaceful Pizza on your Palate

Q -Quest for Quality

R -Read & Rhyme

S -Stay Strong and Sing a Song

T -Time to Try Thankfulness

U -Use the Universe to Unite

V -Vivaciously Value Victory

W -Win in the World

X -Sail the Xebec and X your name to make your fame

Y -Yours will be Yummy

Z -Zeal will keep it real

Chapters of Chef Tomato's Expedition 1-8

1. The Pepperoni Planet

2. Sweet Spinning Spinach Slopes

3. A Journey Through the Milky Way

4. Across the Sea on the Cheese Block

5. A Shake Between Two Hands

6. Look At the Sign: We are on Top

7. The Masterpiece and the Miracle Magic Music Box

8. Making the Dough For the End of the Show

Chapter 1

The Pepperoni Planet

Tom Hart

As the sun rises in the morning, Master Chef Tomato heats the oven using solar powered energy, so he can get the pizzas flying out of the building. Tomato knows that all the children start to have lunch around noon. Once all the dough is made, he starts to prepare the sauce. He slices the tomatoes, onions, peppers and his favorite ingredient in the universe, garlic. While Tomato finishes making the red marinara sauce and cutting all the fresh vegetables picked today in the garden, the rest of the kitchen staff works hard and diligently to they can make the world's best pizza pie. The whole team has worked together in a great environment where they strive to achieve excellence and bring forth a world of joy.

Saving our planet from one piece of pizza will give everyone hope for a sustainable promised land.

Chef Tomato and his crew decide on the pizza of the day. They choose fresh mozzarella, fresh basil, and Tomato's secret pizza sauce and the most delicious pepperoni on the planet. Now that is a pizza pie. Perfection is guaranteed with this pizza.

There is a great smell in the air and the finished pizzas come out of the brick oven. Crisp, light and soft dough complement the wonderful toppings of the pizza. Clearly, through the skies of the Pepperoni Planet, Chef Tomato makes the best pizza pies.

Everyone can make great pizzas. So start today and follow Tomato's way!

Pizza Dough Recipe

Universal Pizza Sauce

Fresh Ingredients

Chapter 2
Sweet Spinning Spinach Slopes

The billboard welcomes everyone to Mushroom Mountain. All the people have their skis on and snowboards ready to go down the slopes. They await a hot slice of pizza as they make their way down the mountain. Many people are looking forward Chef Tomato's Team for delicious pizzas with all the toppings. They have so much room on the mountain that the Starship sends all the pizzas down the slope for all to enjoy.

A touch of honey adds a little sweetness to the crust. The floral notes of honey give the dough a lovely flavor. The freshness of the pizzas warms everyone on the mountain so they can continue to slide along the slopes. These are the best pizzas from all over the universe. The Starship has a pizza oven and all the freshest ingredients to make any kind of pizza. One of the most popular Pizzas that the Team makes is The White Snow Top Pizza. It has Ricotta and Mozzarella Cheeses, Spinach, Roasted Garlic, Fresh Basil and Olive Oil. The Recipe Follows:

Chapter 3

A Journey Through the Milky Way

There are many different ways to top a pizza. The first and most important is the sauce. Using your freshest and most enjoyed vegetables and herbs will help deliver a great sauce. Chef Tomato has given you one of the best recipes in the Universe. Have fun cooking!

The Universal Pizza Sauce

- Red Peppers ½ c diced (Optional Ingredient)

- Vidalia (Sweet) Onion ½ c diced

- Garlic ⅛ c chopped

- Crushed Tomatoes 1lb

- Tomato Paste ¼ c

- Basil (fresh) 4 tbs

- Oregano (fresh) 2 tbs

- Red Pepper Flakes (for a kick) 1 tbs

- Salt and Pepper pinch of each

To make the sauce, on medium heat, sauté with 2 tbs olive oil, the peppers, onion and garlic for 5 minutes. Then add the tomatoes and tomato paste, stir and finish the sauce by adding the fresh herbs, salt and pepper. Continue to simmer sauce on low heat for two hours and stir often to prevent it from burning. Allow to cool before adding sauce to the pizza.

Chapter 4

Across the Sea on the Cheese Block

Sailing the globe and making pizzas is Chef Tomato's dream. He believes peace and be reached by making great dough and sharing a slice with everyone on the planet. As he sails across the sea he delivers everyone a peaceful treat. . Is that the secret? Share a slice of pizza and your peaceful spirit will be enjoyed. Chef Tomato travels the world finding peace within everyone. You should try too.

It's all about You & Pizza (Now we will make world peace!)

The style of you makes your slice great.

A journey of two to make everyone a great pizza

An awesome pizza race to travel the world

What other people like is a personal choice.

We make our choices based upon our moral decisions and great dreams

Whether neighbors or pen pals miles away, we all unite and bring the world love, hope, and peace through pizza making.

Chapter 5

A Shake Between Two Hands

A long time ago the world decided through time that everyone must find some way of connecting and developing a sign of peace. No weapons here. On earth the human race joins together in a shake between two hands. If you haven't tried it, Chef Tomato recommends the toasted marshmallow chocolate malt. When we meet for the first time or the last, people shake each other's hand to say hello and goodbye. By acknowledging each other's worth we are guided to discover friendship.

Shakes are so easy to make. They can be made with any source of goodness. Chef loves his Madagascar vanilla and sweet tart cherry flavors. The recipes follow as they will make anyone excited to shake your hand once they have tasted all the goodness in the glass. Ice cold and scrumptious. May all enjoy a great shake!

Milkshakes Made Easy

- Combine all ingredients in a blender and blend to a smooth consistency. Now that was easy!

Milkshake Recipes

1. The Chubby Monkey Chocolate Cookie

    - ⅛ cup chocolate syrup
    - 1 fresh banana
    - ¼ cup half and half
    - 2 scoops vanilla ice cream
    - 2 scoops chocolate ice cream
    - 4 Oreo cookies

    Mix all ingredients in blender for a smooth concoction.

2. Fresh Berry Fields Forever

   - ¼ cup blueberries
   - ¼ cup blackberries
   - ¼ cup strawberries
   - ¼ cup raspberries
   - 2 scoops vanilla ice cream
   - 2 scoops strawberry ice cream
   - ¼ cup half and half

   Mix all ingredients in blender for a smooth berry blend.

3. Coffee Colossal Grand Daddy

   - ⅛ cup Powdered malt
   - ⅛ cup coffee syrup
   - 4 Scoops coffee ice cream
   - ¼ cup half and half

   Blend together and garnish with whipped cream and dust with malt and toasted walnuts.

4. Journey through the Milky Way

   - 2 Milky Way bars (or your favorite candy bars)
   - ⅛ cup half and half or milk
   - 4 scoops vanilla bean ice cream
   - 2 tablespoons caramel sauce
   - 2 tablespoons chocolate syrup

   Mix all ingredients in blender for a smooth milkshake.

5. Sublime Lime Time Crunch

    *   4 Scoops Lime sherbet
    *   2 teaspoons vanilla extract
    *   2 tablespoons caramel syrup
    *   ⅛ cup half and half

    Mix all ingredients in blender for a smooth sublime shake.

    Add whipped cream and sprinkle with Peppermint candies (crushed for a crunch)

6. The Rock and Roll Toasted Marshmallow

    *   8 Medium Toasted or Untoasted Marshmallows (One cup of marshmallow cream is equivalent)

    *   4 Scoops chocolate or vanilla ice cream

    *   ⅛ cup caramel syrup

    *   ⅛ cup chocolate syrup

    *   ¼ cup half and half

    Mix all ingredients in blender for a smooth delicious delight

    Garnish with crushed graham crackers, chocolate chips, and walnuts.

Chapter 6

Look At the Sign: We are on Top

The world spins fast. Days go by without everyone knowing each other. We are guided by the light of the sun and this is our sign of peace. The world has so many activities to offer. It is time to make a difference and it is time to make world peace. People of all ages need to know there is a way for peace can be recognized. This is the sign of hope and a sign of peace. The peace sign stands for unity and a time where everyone joins together. A global strategy for unity is forever as we all shall need to be nice and have a slice of peace. See it's not that we can't solve the issue, but rather we all want our liberties. Now since peace has been accomplished we are on top. Our lives are vital to strong relationships among nations. Look at the sign, now you see? Here is our chance to shine and make a difference. The sky is the limit and we will all be on top!

Peacefully Enter The Top For Your Prize of Peace!

Topping Ideas

Pizza Crust

Thin,Thick, Deep Dish, Hand Tossed

Pizza Sauce

Tomato, BBQ, Buffalo, White Garlic, Alfredo, Ranch, Balsamic Glaze

Cheese

Mozzarella, Provolone, Cheddar, Goat Cheese, Parmesan, Feta, Blue Cheese, Ricotta

Vegetables

Peppers, Oniion, Olives, Sundried Tomatoes, Spinach, Mushrooms, Pineapple, Garlic, Eggplant, Broccoli, Figs, Zucchini, Fresh Herbs

Meats

Pepperoni, Sausage, Ham, Proscuitto, Salami, Roast Beef, Bacon, Chicken (buffalo, bbq, parmesan, jerk, roasted)

Chapter 7

The Masterpiece and the Miracle
Magic Music Box

The master chef Tomato and his team have decided that when every box travels through the universe, not only will be pizza box be delivered, but a beautiful symphony of music will be released from the Miracle Magic Music Box. Sing along to the song because the pizza makes miracles come true. Whether or not the sound of music travels along into space, making pizza is fun and rewarding. Though one thing is for sure, your pizza can have as many topping as possible. Everyone travels through the cosmos and the beauty of the Miracle Magic Music Box is that Tomato has provided the best recipes so any one can make his creations.

Here are some of Tomato's words of advice.

The sound of hope will guide everyone along into their dreams which will make life better for all.

The belief of the world should be for a peaceful land where everyone gets a chance to shine like a star.

Glow as you please for the light at night is only here for so long.

Take the chance to reinvent yourself; take on the challenge of our destiny for as long as your heart directs your guidance.

Dream Big, Go Far, See The Beauty In The Peaceful World

Chapter 8

Making the Dough For the End of the Show

Art is shown in so many forms. Everyone has an artistic side and they should show off their skills. This is the art of making great pizza dough. Tomato's pizza dough has only 5 ingredients to make a delicious pie. Anyone can make it. That's right: in the world of peace and in the oven. It is easy to make. One day an order for one thousand pizzas was called into Chef Tomato's pizzeria castle. Never before has he received an order so large. Luckily Chef Tomato had been making dough all day. Chef Tomato made everyone happy just like you can for your family and friends with just one piece of pizza. Helping others is the key for future prosperity and fortune. If everyone in the world had a helping hand once in a while they would show how we all can make the dough. Bringing about love and making each other happy, are key elements of being peaceful. This is your contribution to solve global peace. We all can make the dough for the end of the show. A peaceful pizza party for everyone.

The Dough Recipe

- 1 ½ teaspoons active dry yeast
- Two tablespoons olive oil
- 1 tablespoon honey (sugar can be a substitute)
- 1 ⅛ cups of water (water should be 110 degrees or warm to the touch)
- 3 cups of all-purpose flour
- 1 ½ teaspoons of salt

To make the dough start with the water oil, honey and yeast and stir together. Allow one minute to go by before adding the flour. Finally add the salt to the dough. You may use a mixer or make by hand in a large bowl. Using a large spoon to stir flour makes for an easy cleanup and assembly. Once dough has formed into a ball. Use an additional amount of flour to knead the dough into balls and allow the dough rest for 20 minutes to rise. Portion the dough for as many pizzas you would like to make. This dough recipe makes 2 large or 4 small pizzas.

Putting the Pizza Together

This pizza dough bakes at 400 degrees Fahrenheit. If you have a pizza stone put it in the oven to heat. Roll the dough out to the thickness you desire. This dough is made to be any size and thickness. Coat a cookie sheet with olive oil and place dough carefully without tearing. Add your favorite sauce and then toppings. Bake In the oven until golden brown crust and let cool before eating. Enjoy your freshly baked pizza.

Quotes

(Great way to have a great day)

Be ready and follow!

The power is in the imagination. For one day that not would be so plentiful than inspiration and thoughts. These ideas will become our future. Think big and have fun.

Let all live free. In a world where all get along. Time for strength and rejoice of all our accomplishments. Since we are here let's all be friends.

Justification is here. We all are equal, yet it is how hard you try that will make the difference.

May the world be able to dream while those who have it all belong united through hope and passion.

Taking upon the world of joy is compromising and demands high energy. May the hopes of all allow for increased levels of greatness that shall encompass spirituality. There is found peace. Let all enjoy.

The life of all will be blessed only if those who respect all will one day gain the best company.

Rise like the sun. A beginning to a bright future can carry on for so many moments. There is time and light in all of us. Beneath the stars are the brightest guides.

Quotes

(Great way to have a great day)

Be ready and follow!

The story will start with the rise of our future. The stars will shine and all will be friends. Take upon the opportunity to strengthen the global network.

For thee we all are united. A space that has determined each others faith must guide our future way of life.

Forever we can last. Now is the future to look at our past and strengthen what we have. There is sound in the world. Hear the sound of peace and may your voice be heard.

Now that change has come about, there is a moment for every person on this peaceful planet. Let's develop a sense of unity.

The universe has created a special kind of light. Star light will make your life bright.

Further into you dream you will see. Climb you way to the sky and then you have flown into a path of beauty and grace.

Let's all travel to see. We will be the people to share all the fun. Together all will be able to unite in a peaceful planet.

The capacity of our dreams must be looked at closely for these times in our lives will bring about enjoyment and a bonding of strength and unity in our community.

Thank You for making a peace & pizza.

The End

About the Author

I am Thomas M. Hart. I have worked extremely hard in the last decade in order to get to where I am now. I have an associates degree in culinary arts and a bachelors degree in food marketing from Johnson and Wales University, Providence, RI. I am inspired from the world and all its offerings. Many great leaders, authors, and musicians before me have opened the doors for my future. With the entire world working together since mankind, I have been able to put my thoughts of peace into this book, "Peace In A World Of Pizza". I am a great chef by trade and hope to share great recipes to an audience of all.

Printed in the United States
By Bookmasters